Something so Big

Story by Martin Waddell
Pictures by Charlotte Canty

OXFORD
UNIVERSITY PRESS

Bill Hooley lived in a pot with his small friends, the Creepies and Crawlies. Each day Something So Big came with the watering can and watered the flowers in the pot. The Creepies and Crawlies all liked that a lot. It stopped them from getting too hot. But one day...

The sun shone and Something So Big didn't come. It got HOT, HOT, HOT, HOT in the pot... almost too hot to breathe...

...much too hot for the Creepies and Crawlies.

4

"Help us, Bill Hooley," they cried, and they curled up like little dried twigs in the shade of the flowers in the pot.

Help us!

5

Bill Hooley was BRAVE.

Tum - tiddy - tum - tiddy - tum - tiddy - tum.

He set off to look for the watering can,
all by his small-self, alone.

Bill Hooley went round Greenbottom's Leaf.
"Good morning, Greenbottom," Bill Hooley said.
"Have you seen the watering can?"
  "You'd better ask Lady Bug," gasped
Greenbottom.

Tum - tiddy

- tum - tiddy - tum - tiddy - tum.

Bill Hooley set off to find Lady Bug,
all by *his* small-self, alone.

9

Bill Hooley climbed up on Lady Bug's branch.
"Good morning Lady Bug," said Bill Hooley.
"Have you seen the watering can?"
    "Beetle might know," Lady Bug panted. "I hope it comes soon."
    So...

Tum - tiddy - tum

- tiddy - tum - tiddy - tum.

...Bill Hooley set off
to find Beetle,
all by his small-self, alone.

11

"Good morning Beetle," Bill Hooley said. "Have you seen the watering can?"
"It might be somewhere over there," Beetle said.

Somewhere-over-there was a long way
to go and Bill Hooley was afraid, but
he HAD to find the watering can,
and so he went on,
all by his small-self,
alone.

Tum - tiddy - tum - tiddy - tum.

Along the Big Root went Bill Hooley.

Around Shiny Leaf went Bill Hooley.

Tum - tiddy - tum - tiddy - tum.

Tum - tiddy - tum - tiddy - tum.

Past Red Flower
went Bill Hooley.

THEN ....

Whoosh

...Bill Hooley was Somewhere-over-there,
where he'd not been before and...
...Bill Hooley was scared,
all by his small-self, alone.

"What's this?" thought Bill Hooley.

"What's that?" thought Bill Hooley.

"What are those?" gasped Bill Hooley.

And then...

17

... "I know what *that is!*" thought Bill Hooley.

It was Something So **Big**, fast asleep.

"I'll tickle it till it wakes up!" thought Bill Hooley. "Then it will water our pot!"

TICKLE, TICKLE, TICKLE...

...and...
Something So **Big**
moved its head.

And then...
Something So **Big**
wiggled its nose.

And then...

Something So **Big** opened one eye.

Something So **Big**
was A-W-A-K-E!

19

"You don't belong here, Little Thing!" yawned Something So Big, looking down at Bill Hooley.

Something So Big put Bill Hooley gently back in the pot. But everything in the pot looked too hot and so...

...Something So **Big** lifted the watering can and...

...WHOOOOOOOOOOOOOSH!

The Creepies and Crawlies all splashed about in the pot.

"You're a hero! You saved us, Bill Hooley!" they cried, and they all danced and flapped round Bill Hooley.

Bill Hooley still lives in the pot with his friends, the Creepies and Crawlies. He likes it a lot because, when it's hot...
Something So **Big** always waters the pot.

...WHOOOOSH!